AFRICAN WILDLIFE

A PORTRAIT OF THE ANIMAL WORLD

JOE MCDONALD

PHOTOGRAPHY BY JOE AND MARY ANN MCDONALD

TODTRI

Acknowledgments

*With the exception of less than a handful of photographs, all of the images
in this book were made in the company of many other photographers,
all of whom accompanied Mary Ann and me on our photo safaris.
Foremost, I'd like to thank those scores of dedicated shooters, whose
patience, enthusiasm, and devotion allowed us to pursue our images.*

*I'd also like to thank the two most important people accompanying
me on safari, my wife Mary Ann, and my head driver,
David Kariithi Ngunyi. Mary Ann's skill as a photographer pushes me
to my own limits, and her companionship and helpfulness makes
our safari life so much easier and more pleasurable. David's skills as a
driver and wildlife observer are without equal, and many of my images
in this book were made under his direction—"Joe, shoot that!"*

This book was designed and produced by
TODTRI Book Publishers
P.O. Box 572, New York, NY 10116-0572
FAX: (212) 695-6984
e-mail: info@todtri.com

Printed and bound in Singapore

ISBN 1-57717-129-2

Author: Joe McDonald

Publisher: Robert M. Tod
Senior Editor: Edward Douglas
Book Designer: Mark Weinberg
Typesetting: Command-O, NYC

Visit us on the web!
www.todtri.com

PHOTO CREDITS

**All photographs © copyright 1999 by
Joe and Mary Ann McDonald
*with the exception of the following:***

Aquila Photographics/Mike Lane, 8–9

Dembinsky Photo Associates/Stan Osolinski, 59

Dembinsky PhotoAssociates/Fritz Polking, 58 (top)

Picture Perfect/Karl Amman, 20 (bottom)

INTRODUCTION

African buffalo sometimes congregate in huge numbers, especially when food or water sources become limited.

From a thousand feet, a Ruppell's vulture spiraled downward on stiff wings, dropping its legs like the landing gear of a strange aircraft as it swept into its final descent. A squabble of over five hundred vultures had preceded it, swarming frantically like feathered maggots over the fresh carcass of a giraffe. The lions that had made the kill had left only an hour earlier, frightened into the brush by the distant sound of Maasai cow bells, and the hyenas that would later dominate the carcass had not yet arrived. The vultures fed feverishly, hissing, creaking, clacking in a hellish witch's brew of noisy, wild clatter.

In decreasing density the vultures fanned out in a rough circle, thickest at the center where scores hopped in and out, sometimes piling on one another's backs as they fought their way into the carcass, thinnest at the edges where the sated, weak, or timid waited their turn. Further out another circle of watchers quietly observed: the tourists, secure in their land rovers and vans.

Life and death, births and killings, triumphs and tragedies, these ancient, timeless, primordial scenes are played out each day in Africa, often within meters of van-loads of fascinated tourists viewing nature, upclose, for the very first time. From the vast plains of East Africa to the forested mountain tops of Uganda and Rwanda, from the waterless red sand deserts of Namibia and the Kalahari to the swamps and marshes of Botswana or the mopani woodlands of Zimbabwe and South Africa, this diverse continent is the home to the most exciting assemblage of animals on earth.

Large carcasses can attract hundreds of vultures at one time. Sometimes as many as four different species may feed at once, with the aggressive Ruppell's vulture often taking the choice feeding spots.

For the wildlife watcher or photographer, nothing can compare to Africa. On a lucky day, even a first-time tourist may spot all of Africa's big cats; the lion, leopard, and cheetah; or the Big Five popular game animals: the buffalo, elephant, black rhino, leopard, and lion. A bird-watcher may tick off 50 species on a game

A group of giraffes at sunset in the Masai Mara.

drive, and 150 to 700 species on a two or three week long safari. There are animals of every description, from beagle-sized antelopes to dinosaur-like crocodilians, elephants that are 13 feet (4 meters) tall and their distant relatives, marmot-like hyraxes. Africa is home to our nearest primate relative, the chimpanzee, and the largest great ape, the mountain gorilla.

Undoubtedly, one of the attractions of wildlife viewing in Africa is the effortlessness in which it can be done. Animals in game reserves and national parks are, in season, easy to find in large numbers, and often big. Certainly that's one of the attractions, for by their very size, elephants, hippopotamuses, rhinos, and giraffes delight the eye and spark the imagination, and if given more than a cursory observation, can treat the viewer to insights into behavior and natural history not possible outside this wildlife-rich continent.

The sheer number of animals is surely another draw. No where else can one find thousands of large animals roaming what appears to be a vast, limitless land. In Kenya and Tanzania, for example, upwards of 1.5 million wildebeest may migrate each year from one grazing ground to another. It's not uncommon in Kruger in South Africa, Etosha in Namibia, the Chobe in Botswana, or Amboseli in Kenya to see several hundred elephants together, feeding, drinking, or marching silently across the land. Seen from the air, Africa's plains are still blackened by the living bodies of thousands of buffalo, or rippled by the striped herds of hundreds of zebra coursing across the grasslands.

Without question, Africa is a most exciting land: the home to an astonishing assortment of mammals, birds, and reptiles. This book tells some of their stories.

The striped pattern on the common zebra differs with each individual. It is suspected that other zebras recognize these unique patterns and use this to distinguish herd relationships.

BASIS OF THE FOOD CHAIN

First-timers on an African safari often are most moved, not by seeing their first lion or elephant, but by the sheer abundance and diversity of the wildlife they're seeing. Sometimes it seems that no matter where you look there are animals. In some areas, zebra, wildebeest, buffalo, or giraffe herds are literally stretched to the horizon, in a pageantry representing practically every size, color, or shape a land mammal can take.

The Grazers

This sense of countless numbers is not misleading. Each year, hundreds of thousands of wildebeest inhabiting the Mara-Serengeti ecosystem travel from their southern calving grounds in Tanzania's lower Serengeti to the rolling grasslands of Kenya's Masai Mara. That spectacle, referred to as "the great migration," is not unique. On smaller scales it is echoed throughout Africa as herbivores seek out new or seasonal grazing sites.

Certainly the most recognizable of these grazers is the zebra. Two species and several subspecies range from southern Ethiopia to the African cape. The Grevy's, the largest zebra, is restricted to semi-desert habitats in northern Kenya, southern Somalia and Ethiopia. It has large donkey-like ears and narrow stripes that end at its belly. More abundant and widespread is the Burchell's, or common, zebra, marked by shorter ears and broader stripes that completely encircle the animal.

Both are herd animals with territorial stallions attempting to keep a harem of mares within their confines. Grevy's zebras, with a much looser social structure, are often found in groups of five or more with females frequently moving between herds. Common zebras maintain much larger harems, which stay intact as they migrate, sometimes in huge herds of hundreds of zebras.

FOLLOWING PAGE: A young elephant, left unguarded, is soon dispatched by a lion's powerful bite into its neck. The sheer weight and strength of the lion is enough to overcome this animal, even though it is larger than the cat.

Young stallions often fight to establish a dominance hierarchy. The zebra stallions bite at each other's hindlegs and, less frequently, rear up on their hind legs to bite and kick. Serious injuries can result if a zebra lands a solid kick to a leg or jaw.

Giraffe fights resemble ritualistic ballets as each animal swings its head in a long arch before pounding the other's side. Although most fights produce few injuries, giraffes have been known to knock each other out during these contests.

Antelope

The antelope of Africa are extremely diverse, representing a huge family, the Bovidae. The patterns, shapes, and markings of this huge group can be so subtle, beginners and experts alike can have trouble telling them apart. Consider the almost bewildering assortment of names: bushbuck, steenbok, springbok, reedbuck, blesbok, waterbuck, dik-dik, kudu, topi, eland, and so on. A few, like the impala, gazelle, or African buffalo have familiar sounding names, while others, like the sitatunga, nyala, or oribi, might challenge the best of scrabble players.

This variety of antelope reflects the many niches each species exploits. In the swamps and marshes of the Okavango, sitatungas travel on long, splayed hooves that prevent the antelope from sinking into the boggy terrain.

Migrating along with wildebeests, zebras are often the first animals to make a river crossing. This is one of the most dangerous times for zebras and wildebeests. In addition to the threat of drowning, both may meet crocodiles in the river and lions lying in ambush along the shoreline.

Two springbok males are dueling. This mid-size antelope gets its name from the high springing jumps, sometimes called stotting or pronking, it makes when danger is spotted.

Gunther's dik-dik inhabits the arid regions of northern Kenya, Uganda, and Somalia. It differs from the similar-looking Kirk's dik-dik by having an unusually long nose.

On the rocky kopjes (or small hills) of the Serengeti, klipspringers nimbly leap from rock to rock, their hooves sharp and blunt, perfect for securing a foothold on even the smallest of ledges. Between these extremes there are lithe, fleet-footed Thompson's and Grant's gazelles; lumbering behemoth-like buffalo; regal horse-like oryx, roan, and sable antelopes; and furtive, seldom-seen bush and forest-dwelling duikers.

The smallest of Africa's antelopes, dik-diks, browse in thickets in semi-arid and grassland habitats in East, Central, and Southwestern Africa. Dik-diks maintain a small home territory they define by prominent dung piles and by scent marking. They are easily overlooked in the underbrush in which they forage, but when they are seen, they are often found in twos or threes—the third being the pair's nearly full-grown offspring. Shy and slinky, a dik-dik might be mistaken for a large African hare as it hop-jumps into cover.

One of the most strikingly patterned antelope is the handsome oryx. With its upright posture and powerful neck, the oryx resembles a horse, and from the side, a unicorn sporting a single horn.

The small klipspringer lives on rocky cliffs, ledges, and kopjes throughout east and southern Africa. Its sharp, blunted hooves are specially adapted for climbing.

Impalas often groom one another's faces and necks, areas impossible to reach for a lone animal.

There'd be no such mistaking the impala, everyone's idea of what an antelope should look like. About the size of the average deer, with clean-looking, two-toned brown hide, a herd of impalas can hardly be missed in the grasslands and open, park-like woodlands they inhabit. Male impalas, especially those defending a harem, can be quite vocal, issuing constant snorts and donkey-like brays. Unlike the dik-dik, impala bucks are polygamous, and

jealously guard their harem from potential suitors. Chasing off rivals and riding herd over a harem of as many as one hundred does can be exhausting, and eventually most resident bucks are displaced by a stronger, fresher buck from a pool of ever-ready bachelors.

Somewhat resembling the impala, the gerenuk is perhaps the most unusual browser in the entire antelope family. Its Swahili name, Swala twiga, or antelope giraffe, best describes it, for the gerenuk has an unusually long neck that reminds one of a giraffe. Gerenuks are unique in standing upon their hind legs to browse, placing one or both forelegs onto adjacent branches for support. In this manner, the gerenuk can browse on a level of vegetation that's higher than most other antelopes, but beneath that of the giraffes'.

The thin, almost wiry stature of a gerenuk stands in marked contrast with the two largest members of the family, the eland and the African buffalo. Eland are true antelopes, but they are huge, standing nearly six feet (2 meters) tall and weighing almost a ton (907 kilograms). Despite their size, eland are tremendous jumpers, able to leap over fences 6 feet (2 meters) high or the backs of other eland when they are in flight.

Gerenuks browse on vegetation that's beyond the reach of the impalas that share their range. To do so, gerenuks stand on their hind legs, balancing themselves by bracing their forelegs upon a small branch.

Bovids

The largest member of this Bovidae family is the huge African buffalo. Gray or black in coloration, with a huge, heavy boss of horn, buffalo are powerful, stocky animals quite capable, when in a group, of facing down a pride of lions. Even single animals are a fair match for any lion, although individuals are often killed by lion prides, especially in the lean times when other, easier prey, are scarce.

Prides and Clans

At sunrise, standing by his kill, a male African lion proclaims his territory. Sounding more like a deep moan than any roar, the lion asks his two-note question, "Who's land?," and answers it with equally deep, but shorter grunts, "Mine!" And in truth, it is, for the lion is the undisputed master of all he surveys on the African plains. Lions are the top predators in the African food chain.

However, in some areas, this claim of top predator can be disputed. In Tanzania's Ngorongoro Crater for example, huge clans of spotted hyenas may claim this title, for in this vast game-rich cauldera, the abundance of hyenas demand they capture their own prey. Roving bands of hyenas capable of tackling adult wildebeests and zebras terrorize the night.

In general, spotted hyenas are considered scavengers, the cleanup team that, to popular notion, lazily or cowardly waits until lions abandon their kills. This perception was, no doubt, generated by field studies made when naturalists were limited to strictly diurnal encounters. Much later, in the 1960s, researchers broadened their scope to include

Because of their long legs and short necks, warthogs must kneel on their forelegs in order to graze. Females may have up to six young, but only a few will survive to adulthood from the attacks of eagles, leopards, and other predators.

Each year thousands of wildebeests, or gnus, travel from Kenya to Tanzania and back again. Although they face many obstacles during the thousand mile journey, none are more threatening than the numerous river crossings they make. Dozens, sometimes even hundreds of animals often drown during the attempt.

nocturnal observations and discovered these roles were occasionally reversed. In the crater, hyenas do most of the hunting, and the lions scavenge.

Lions, the only true social cats, live in prides, usually comprised of two or three generations of related females, their young male offspring, and their cubs. At the head of the pride are from one to four males in the prime of their life.

Male Lions

At age three, young males are generally forced out of the pride by the resident males. For the next few years, the young males mature, developing into powerful adversaries, until at age five or six, they are ready to claim a pride of their own.

While a lone challenger may be unsuccessful in besting the resident pride male or males, coalitions are sometimes formed by several males of similar ages and these coalitions often win. In some contests, depending upon the health and age of the resident males, vicious battles determine the outcome. In others, the resident males intuitively understand the odds, and without even a snarl turn tail and run.

The resident lionesses may not immediately accept the new pride masters. In extreme cases, this reluctance can so fragment the cohesiveness of the pride that it dissolves. But the new males are insistent on establishing

Mating lions can be very active. In the first day or two the lions may copulate every twenty minutes or so, averaging two matings per hour over a four or five day honeymoon.

Social contact is important with lions. Lionesses invariably bump heads together when they meet, and cubs constantly intertwine themselves around their mother, often sliding right beneath her chin.

Lions are swift and efficient killers. They either strangle their victims by an attack on the throat or suffocate them by covering the mouth and nostrils.

To obtain such a favored food as a warthog, pride teamwork is used to surround the creature's burrow and wait patiently. When the animal begins to emerge, the group pounces forward to dig it out of the ground and subdue it.

their new role and passing along their genes to new generations.

To do so obviously requires receptive females. Lactating females or those with young cubs will not be in estrus in the near future, so to facilitate their receptiveness, the new males practice infanticide by killing the young offspring of the former resident males. When the females finally do accept their presence in the pride, they go into heat, the males mate, and a new lineage is formed.

Pride males are often accused of having an easy life, since lionesses make the kills which the males often steal, only abandoning the kills when they are sated. Superficially this is true, but the males' roles are more complex and dangerous than that.

Once pride ownership is established, it is the males that maintain the pride's territory. This can involve heated, even deadly, confrontations with other male lions. Male lions are invaluable in protecting kills from marauding hyenas, a role especially important during the lean dry seasons. And, although males often drive the females off a kill, they are tolerant of their cubs. Genetically, this makes sense, since by sharing kills with their cubs, the males help to insure that their young will survive their early years.

The length of reign for most resident males is relatively short. By age six or seven, most male lions lose possession of their pride to younger, stronger rivals. Some may do so unscathed, while others may be crippled, maimed, or mortally wounded in the process. Either way, a big male lion will be taxed to find enough food on his own to sustain his bulk. Most males are not long-lived.

A pride of lions alertly drinks at a water hole. This spot is favored by many other animals, but as the lions arrive, all will leave.

On occasion, lionesses may fan out to circle their prey from several directions, capturing their victim after a long stalk and a short, lightning fast charge, often beginning within 20–30 yards (18–27 meters). But where a lion may give up a chase after a 100 yards (90 meters) or less, hyenas may run for miles if success seems likely. Their natural loping gate stretches to a gallop, and they move with a seemingly tireless pace.

Once the prey is stopped, hyenas begin feeding, ripping first into the soft underbelly of their prey until shock or loss of blood drops the animal. With the most powerful jaws in nature, hyenas are capable of crushing all but the largest bones, and even these will be carried off to be gnawed on at a later date. Their jaws are so strong, and their metabolism so efficient, that hyenas can even make a meal of old bones

Despite their differences, the fact that both lions and hyenas are social animals has undoubtably contributed to their abundance and visibility. There's safety and security in numbers, and while neither species is the most abundant or widespread African predator, they play a prominent role on the plains of the African savannah.

After stripping the flesh from a buffalo's ribcage, this hyena walked off with a length of vertebrae nearly as long as its body.

Hyenas

In hyena clans, conversely, females dominate. Oddly, females, even those that are nursing, superficially resemble males by possessing an elongated clitoris resembling a penis. Like lions, female hyenas generally remain with their birth clan, while males leave after their second year.

Though both lions and hyenas are social animals, when hunting, neither plans a strategy.

Very young spotted hyenas are coal black. Adults set up a communal den where pups of several ages may gather to play.

Giraffes are at their most vulnerable when drinking, and a giraffe may take several minutes before attempting a drink. Because its forelegs and shoulders are taller than its neck is long, a giraffe must position itself in an awkward, wide-open spread-eagle to reach the water.

PREDATORS LARGE AND SMALL

Arguably, two of the most beautiful big cats in the world, leopards and cheetahs, share few similarities. Both, of course, are spotted, and both are approximately the same size and weight, but there are significant differences between the two.

Leopards

Leopards spend the day sleeping, waking up in late afternoon to begin their hunt.

A leopard's coat is composed of both singular spots and clusters, arranged in a ring-like or rosette pattern, while the cheetah's coat is only spotted. Although approximately the same weight, their physical structure is markedly different. Leopards are robust, heavy shouldered cats built for short dashes and for

Off all the big cats, the leopard is most at home in trees and regularly sleeps high off the ground. The cubs learn to climb at an early age and are left in trees for their own saftey while their mother is off hunting.

dragging prey into trees. Cheetahs are lithe, greyhound-like felines capable of speeds exceeding that of any other land mammal.

Leopards literally pounce upon their prey, slithering like a spotted shadow until they're within a few yards, or even a few feet, of their victim. Successful hunts are likely to be on motionless or slow moving animals that are literally rolled by the force of the leopard's charge.

Cheetahs

Cheetahs chase their prey, usually by stalking within 50–70 yards (45–65 meters). Cheetahs are sprinters, and for short distances they can reach speeds of at least 50 miles-(80 kilometers-) per-hour. With their long tails used as a rudder for balance, and non-retractable claws, unique in the cat family, cheetahs can follow nearly any move their fleeing prey may make. Prey is captured either when it falls, by losing its footing in a tight turn, or when tripped by the cheetah's outstretched forepaw. On the back of this forepaw is a recurved claw, called a dew claw, which is used as a hook in the trip-

From her position in a low tree, this leopardess can survey the countryside for prey. Should her hunt be successful, the leopardess will drag her prey up into a tree where it will be safe from marauding hyenas.

The facial markings of each cheetah are distinctive and are a means researchers use to identify individuals in their study areas.

Leopards are the most opportunistic of all the big cats and will capture animals as small as mice or as large as small zebras. Baby warthogs are a favorite.

Young cheetahs learn to hunt by chasing stunned or injured prey brought back to them by their mother. In chases lasting for nearly 100 yards (90 meters), these young cheetahs successfully tackled this Thompson's gazelle several times, although they had not yet learned how to kill the animal they caught.

An alert cheetah, neck stretched for a better view, prepares to run after its prey. It will wait until the right moment before making its high-speed dash.

ping process. However, if they aren't successful within the first few hundred yards, they must stop, rest, and cool down. Even when successful, cheetahs generally spend several minutes just lying beside their kill, panting, before they begin to feed.

The prey they feed upon differs as well. As much as any hungry predator can be a specialist, cheetahs primarily feed on antelope and their young and African hares. The young of zebras, wildebeests, and other antelope are occasionally taken as well.

Feeding Differences

Leopards in contrast are generalists, feeding upon any protein they find, including carrion. Their favorite prey includes young antelope, especially impalas, as well as monkeys, warthogs, snakes, dogs, jackals, or birds—just about anything they're big enough or lucky enough to kill.

To protect their kills from being stolen by hyenas or lions, leopards cache their prey in the branches of trees. Leopards are perhaps the strongest of all the cats, and are capable of carrying even an adult impala weighing over 100 pounds (45 kilograms) 20 feet (6 meters) up into a tree. Cheetahs rarely, if ever, eat anything that they do not kill, but leopards, in contrast, will steal a cheetah's kill at every opportunity, as will hyenas and lions. Consequently, cheetahs often kill midday when other predators are resting in the shade.

Cheetahs are the fastest land mammals on earth. Although it was once thought that cheetahs could sprint at up to 70 miles-(112 kilometers-) per-hour, new evidence suggests their top speed may be 30 percent less.

Hazards to Survival

In the 1970s a fashion craze endangered all the world's spotted cats from overhunting and from poaching. Although cheetahs are still endangered, their vulnerability is due to habitat loss and to an odd genetic constriction. It's believed that cheetahs suffered two major population crashes in prehistory, so reducing their numbers that all cheetahs today are essentially twins, sharing the same DNA and putting them at risk for a disease or virus to spread catastrophically through their ranks.

The more adaptable leopard has recovered from these earlier population losses, and while not immune to the ramifications of habitat loss, their numbers are healthy.

The Lesser Predators

Besides the big cats and hyenas, Africa is home to numerous smaller predators, from cats half the size of a leopard to mongooses barely larger than a mouse. One of these, the spotted serval is an inhabitant of high country moors and grassy savannahs. About the size of a bobcat, servals are most active at night, early morning, and dusk. Days are spent nestled within a thick tussock of grass where their cryptic pattern makes them all but invisible.

Banded mongooses are among the most social of the many species found in Africa. Bands of as many as fifty roam the grasslands seeking insects and birds nests, and taking shelter from danger inside termite mounds and warthog burrows.

The cheetah's strong jaws clamp tightly around the neck of a Thompson's gazelle, preventing it from escaping and quickly suffocating it. Later, the prey will be ripped open by powerful canine teeth.

Caracals are the largest of the small cats. Because it is frequently found in semi-arid areas and sports long ear tufts, its sometimes known as the desert lynx.

The Smaller Cats

Servals are prodigious leapers, hunting much like the American coyote, pinpointing their prey with huge, dish-like ears, then leaping in a high arch to pin their prey beneath their forepaws. They're excellent mousers, but also eat birds, insects, and frogs.

A similarly big-eared cat is the caracal, or African lynx. Although their ears are only slightly larger than a typical cat's, each is tipped with long hairs that exaggerate their length, providing the lynx-like appearance. Caracals are the largest of the small cats, a large male weighing 40 pounds (18 kilograms), and they are extremely powerful for their size, capable of killing adult impalas.

Canine Killers

A desert and open country canine, the little bat-eared fox also shares this big-eared characteristic, using its huge ears like a radar dish to home in on burrowing insects. Hearing one, the fox churns up the soil with its forelegs to uncover its prey.

Bat-eared foxes are primarily nocturnal. Besides insects, they'll also feed upon rodents, reptiles, and nesting birds. Bat-eared foxes are tiny, weighing about 10 pounds (4.5 kilograms) and standing 1 foot (30 centimeters) tall and two feet (60 centimeters) long.

Although there are several species of jackals, the black-backed, or silver-backed, jackal is the most common. They are frequently seen around lion or hyena kills. Fast, alert, and seemingly fearless, a jackal will stay just out of range of a lion or hyena, and when the opportunity arises, dart in to steal a bite.

Black-backs are also efficient predators. Working in pairs with their mate or their older young, they represent a serious threat to small antelopes during the birthing season. Jackals criss-cross the grasslands methodically, sniffing out or flushing well camouflaged babies huddled in the grass.

Wild Dogs

The now critically endangered African wild dog, or Cape hunting dog, was once found throughout much of central and southern Africa. Perhaps of all the predators the wild dog is the most efficient, hunting in packs to run down its prey. Their natural tenacity, coupled with small jaws not suited to quickly dispatch prey, earned the wild dog an almost pathological enmity amongst farmers, hunters, and even some conservationists in former times. They were shot, poisoned, and persecuted wherever they were found.

In early morning, especially on overcast days, adult bat-eared foxes and their pups can be found around their den. Because of the pups' tiny size, adults always keep a sharp eye out for predators.

Taking a break from feeding at their kill, two African wild dogs engage in play, wrestling one another and boxing.

Indeed, wild dogs are frighteningly efficient. A day's hunt begins at sunrise when the air is still cool and a long, drawn out sprint isn't too taxing. Then, two or more dogs begin to mill about, yelping and squealing, submissively greeting one another in what's been likened to a pep rally. Eventually the dogs set off, heading to the nearest game herd. Once there, the dogs begin trotting, frightening their prey into a run that allows them to select the weakest or slowest antelope, wildebeest, or zebra.

The dogs have incredible stamina, and can run seemingly flat out for as long as it takes, although in truth, they often run in relays, and by doing so, wear down their prey. Like hyenas, dogs catch their prey anywhere they can lock on, but their favorite grip is at the muzzle where one dog holds fast while the others begin tearing at the hind quarters and belly.

Like the North American wolves that have suffered similar persecution, wild dogs are now viewed differently, not in anthropomorphic terms but in their role as predators in their world. Researchers and photographers who have spent time with African wild dogs know them as endearing creatures, devoted to their young and to their pack. Despite this turn about in public perception, and their official status as an endangered species, the African wild dog's future seems bleak. Canine distemper and rabies regularly wipe out populations whenever they come into contact with man. In the Masai Mara and northern Tanzania, Maasai herdsmen's dogs have, through their diseases, virtually eliminated the dogs from what was once prime habitat.

After a lone hyena left the carcass, a pair of black-backed jackals moved in, gulping down the remaining meat to take back to their young. Once weaned, pups at the den are fed meat regurgitated by both parents.

A large but seldom seen resident of deserts and grasslands of southern Africa, brown hyenas sport an unusually long-haired coat.

IMPOSING GIANTS, FORBIDDING LANDSCAPES

For many on safari, the African elephant is their favorite animal; that preference resulting from actually watching elephants in the field, not from any pre-trip anticipation of seeing the largest land mammal on earth. While many anxiously await seeing their first male lion, which sleeps during their entire encounter, the animation of the elephant comes as a pleasant surprise.

Elephants

Elephants live in herds of ten to twenty individuals, composed of one or more elder females, the matriarchs that lead the group, their daughters and sisters, and their young. Sometimes several family groups travel together, and herds of seventy to two hundred elephants are not uncommon. Male elephants leave the herd as teenagers. Adult bulls are usually solitary, or pair up with other bulls, and only join the females' herd when they're seeking out a mate.

Elephant groups, even when some distance apart, keep in contact with each other through a variety of sounds, some of which are at such a low frequency that they're inaudible to the human ear. Before the discovery of these subsonic rumbles, bewildered researchers, watching elephants miles apart apparently

Elephants feed both day and night. An elephant may eat over 600 pounds (270 kilograms) of grass, tree bark, saplings, and other vegetative matter in twenty-four hours.

Large tusked elephants are rare today as poaching for the valuable ivory has eliminated most big tuskers. In many areas, elephant tusks are rather short, worn or broken in their efforts to find food.

responding to the same signals, entertained the possibility that elephants might be psychic. Nothing else seemed to explain the coordinated movements of these animals downwind and out of sight of each other.

Herd contact is important, and it's rare to see a lone female or subadult. When elephants meet, they extend their trunks upward and often times caress each other's faces, or place their trunks into each other's mouths.

The trunk is the elephant's most unique feature, the ultimate tool for exploiting its many habitats and food sources. Powered by 150,000 separate muscles, the trunk serves as a nose, a hose, a snorkel, a trumpet, a hand, an arm,

and a battering ram! Its uses, if instinctive, are not automatic, and it's truly comical to watch a baby elephant run, its trunk inscribing dizzying circles as it takes on an uncontrolled inertia.

Elephants often use their trunk in conjunction with their tusks to break tree limbs, laying the branch across one tusk for extra leverage. The elephant's tusks are an extension of its canine teeth. Tusks grow throughout the elephant's life, but few tusks ever reach their full length, snapping off due to wear or, in the case of males, fighting. A big tusker, then, does not imply a bull; a cow elephant feeding on grasses or other soft tissues may have enormous tusks.

Unfortunately, it is the ivory from the tusk of the elephant that has proven to be its greatest liability. Throughout Africa and Asia, where law enforcement is lax and poverty widespread, poachers have decimated elephants in their unlawful pursuit of this lucrative commodity.

The Horned Giant

Africa's second largest mammal, the rhinoceros, has suffered similarly from poaching—not for ivory but for its horn, which is prized by some peoples for its supposedly aphrodisiac properties. In truth, the horn of a rhino isn't a horn at all but is merely an outgrowth of the skull composed of compacted keratinous material, the same substance that comprises human fingernails and hair.

Unlike elephants that use their tusks to assist in procuring food, a rhino's horn serves only as ornamentation, or as a weapon. At one time, these horns grew to enormous lengths of 40 inches (1 meter) or longer, especially in the black rhino, but most of the rhinos sporting these horns have been poached.

Of the five rhinocerous species worldwide, two live in Africa, the black and the white. Their names have little to do with their color, although the former are generally a dark slate gray and may have earned its name from its color. Tannish gray to mid-gray in color, white rhinos get their name from the Afrikaans or Dutch word, *weit*, describing the shape of their broad, wide mouths. White rhinos are grazers using their "weit" mouths for munching

FOLLOWING PAGE: Elephants will test each other in friendly wrestling matches. By doing so, they can frequently avoid serious conflicts, since individuals are aware of each other's strengths.

Two white rhinos square off, contesting a female that grazes nearby.
The most dangerous time for any fight is when one of the two has had enough.
When that rhino turns to flee, it is vulnerable to attack from the sides or back.

grasses close to the ground. Black rhinos, in contrast, are browsers, with a triangular-shaped upper lip that's used for plucking leaves from brush.

Due to poaching, both species are rare today, although the white rhinoceros's numbers have increased significantly from their historic lows. Those of black rhinos have not, and with an almost uncontrolled bout of poaching that began in the 1960s, and continues to this day, their numbers have plummeted from nearly 70,000 in 1960 to less than 2,200 today.

Water Giants

When, not too long ago, most visitors to the remote areas of Africa were hunters seeking trophies, elephants and black rhinoceroses were considered two of the "Big Five," the ultimate and most dangerous of African trophies. It comes as a surprise, then, to discover that the harmless-looking hippopotamus may be the most dangerous mammal in Africa. A denizen of rivers, lakes, and ponds, the hippopotamus is a grazer, but it does not feed in the waters where it dwells. Instead, the nocturnal hippo leaves the protection of the

water each night to travel as far as two or more miles in search of pastures.

Because they may forage far from their diurnal havens, hippos sometimes return to their ponds or streams after sunrise, when local villagers are making their own pilgrimage to water. Hippos are bad-tempered, and crossing one's path on its return trip could prove extremely hazardous.

Although all hippos yawn, bulls frequently do so as a display of dominance. Hippo bulls are quite intolerant of one another and will fight if their yawning displays are unheeded.

Baby hippos are tiny replicas of the adults. The mother pays careful attention to her baby, guarding it from the aggressive bulls.

The triangular lip of the black rhino is used to pluck leaves from low growing bushes and shrubs.

Favoring cliffs, rock outcrops, and granite kopjes, rock hyraxes can be found throughout much of central and southern Africa. They often live in small groups, and in the early morning hours may be found bunched together for warmth.

Hippos are territorial too, and boaters drifting down rivers may be capsized by an angry bull defending its turf or harem. Although not equipped with a rhino's long horn or an elephant's tusk, the hippo's long canine teeth, or tushes, are fiercesome weapons. Often measuring over one foot in length, the tushes are flat sided, forming a scissors-like shearing surface where the upper and lower canines meet. Caught between them, a man could be sawed in two in almost as many bites.

Although they forage on land, hippos are truly an aquatic mammal, mating in the water and giving birth in shallow water or on a nearby shore. Their young are tiny, weighing 50–120 pounds (22–55 kilograms), but they are adorable miniatures of the adults, which weigh 3,500–7,000 pounds (1,590–3,180 kilograms). Babies nurse underwater, closing their ear and nostril openings when they do so, returning to the surface every few seconds to breathe.

Harsh Habitats

Not all of Africa's wildlife is found on the broad grassy savannahs of East Africa, or the mopane woodlands of south-central and southern Africa. Indeed, great wildlife viewing is available in a diverse range of habitats, but perhaps none is more surprising than the austere, enchanting landscapes of the Kalahari, Etosha, and the Namib desert.

Kalahari

The fauna of the Kalahari is aptly represented by that found in the sprawling Gemsbok-Kalahari National Park, tucked in the north-western corner of South Africa and Gemsbok National Park in southern Botswana. Red sands form low, undulating dunes flanking pans of often withered grasses and acacia thickets where, in the dry season, mammals

In the deserts, African ground squirrels seek out seeds, edible grasses, and insects. On hot afternoons they often use their brushy tails as a source of shade.

A tiny shovel-nosed lizard faces down a potential threat. Such occurrences are rare, as the lizard normally flees, running across the sands with surprising speed, before diving beneath the sand and "swimming" a few inches beneath its surface to hide.

congregate at the few precious water holes. Despite the aridity, gemsbok and springbuck are common, prey for lesser numbers of cheetahs and magnificent black-maned lions.

Etosha

Located in north central Namibia, Etosha, the place of dry water, is a study in contrasts. During the December–January rainy season, the pan fills, and the surrounding flatlands explode in soft, pastel green new growth. Flamingos gather by the thousands to feed in the alkaline water, and resident game disperses to the far corners of the park, free with the promise of abundant water sources.

By June, the height of the dry season, backcountry waterholes are largely gone, and the vast, shallow lake is now a salty plain, etched by the meandering tracks of zebras and oryx, and stirred by white, swirling dust devils. Etosha's few permanent waterholes become the daily rendezvous for southern giraffe, Chapman's zebra, greater kudu, wildebeest, springbok, and Etosha's huge herds of elephants.

Elephants love water, and that's clearly evident in their exuberance as they make their final sprint across the flats, kicking up vast white clouds of chalk-like dust. It also shows in the way they play: rolling, splashing, and spraying until their white-coated hides shine blackly in the late afternoon light.

So different is the approach of the smaller herbivores, even those the size of a giraffe 18 feet (5.5 meters) tall. A giraffe approaching a waterhole is a study in patience. Whether alone or with a group of twenty or more, the giraffe proceeds slowly, stopping to scan the horizon periodically before it arrives at the water's edge. Once there, it pauses, sometimes for minutes on end, before tentatively dipping its head and splaying its legs as if to drink. The giraffe is most vulnerable when drinking, and it may jerk upright several times before it determines no predator is near and feels secure enough to lower its head to finally drink.

The Skeleton Coast

West and south of Etosha lies some of Africa's most arid and forbidding landscapes: the ominously named Skeleton coast and the Namib-Naukluft Park. Thick fogs created by the interface of the cold Atlantic Ocean current and the desert-heated air provide the only reliable moisture for animals inhabiting this land of sweeping sand dunes. Beetles have adapted to drinking the fog droplets that collect upon their carapaces by elevating their hind end and allowing the moisture to trickle forward. Namib chameleons, barking geckos, shovelnosed lizards, and Peringuey's vipers have adopted similar water-gathering or water-saving techniques.

A group of southern giraffes bend to drink at a waterhole in Hwange National Park, Zimbabwe. Greater kudu, sable antelope, impala, wildebeests, and Chapman's zebras are common here.

Chapman's zebra, a subspecies of the common zebra, cluster by the hundreds at a waterhole in Etosha. The animals are nervous, for they are most vulnerable to predators at these locations.

In the granite out-crops of the Namib-Naukluft, many birds, reptiles, and small mammals find safety. In sheltered ledges and shallow caves bushmen lived, and their paintings can still be found in undisturbed locations.

Once lions stalked the beaches of the Skeleton coast, feeding upon the Cape fur seals that haul up onto these beaches to breed. The lions are gone, but the fur seals remain, and at Cape Cross up to 200,000 seals gather to breed and give birth each year, making this the largest concentration of seals in Africa.

Amongst this herd, black-backed jackals thread, seeking the rare unguarded or injured pup, and, for a few short weeks, the discharged placentas from the seal cows.

The Namib Desert

In the desolate landscape of the Namib Desert, dominated by shifting, towering white and red sand dunes, one wouldn't expect to find large plant eaters, but the beautifully marked gemsbok or southern oryx are at home amongst the tallest dunes, those in Sossusvlei. There is no standing water in Sossusvlei, which is named for the beautiful pan, or lake, that forms amidst the dunes every few years when rain drops sufficient moisture.However, the oryx derives sufficient water year round by eating the nara plant, a type of pumpkin with melon-like fruit, which survives this harsh environment by means of a deep tap root that finds deep moisture beneath this arid land.

In the towering sand dunes of Sossusvlei, gemsbok, or southern oryx, wander between the dunes seeking melons and dry grasses. The gemsbok rarely drinks, getting its moisture from the plants it eats.

These crescent sand dunes in the Namib-Naukluft desert may, in time, bury the camel tree acacias growing nearby. The sand dunes are dynamic, and change shape dramatically in only a few years.

A WEALTH OF SPECIES

A guide leads a group of tourists, who have been trekking for three hours, up and along the steep, sparsely wooded hillsides of Bwindi National Park's impenetrable forest, following the spoor of one of two habituated gorilla groups. Starting at the gorillas' nests from the previous night, the tour group had followed their meandering route, passing through both open meadows and tracks of darkened forests. Gradually, they are aware of a pungent odor like horse manure and very ripe underarms. Flies cluster thickly on several trailside leaves. The guide places his finger to his lips, gesturing for silence.

Pok! Pok! Pok-pok-pok-pok-pok! The hollow drumbeat of a silverback echoes through the mountain forest, and the tourists wait with nervous anticipation. Suddenly a thin leaf-covered branch shakes and bends, and a black hand and arm appears amidst the vegetation. The guide points, not at the arm, but at another blackened hulk sitting unnoticed 30 feet (9 meters) away.

Sitting on his haunches, supported by one massive arm, the silverback scratches its belly lazily, his gaze directed further up the hill. A female joines the silverback, stepping out of the screening vegetation for a second, then disappearing once more. With a rolling heave the male rises to all fours and follows. Only then are the human observers aware of their racing heart beats.

Gorilla trekking, though sometimes arduous, provides one of the most intimate and exciting wildlife viewing opportunities available in Africa. Gorillas have a mystique, a sometimes frightening glamour fostered by sci-fi films and early, inaccurate "white hunter"

The silverback is the most experienced and knowledgeable gorilla in the group. The rest of the group is composed of several mature females and their young of various ages, including maturing males and females.

documentaries. True, a silverback may charge intruders, including gorilla trekkers, but almost all charges are bluff. Still, that moment, for those who have experienced it, is truly unforgettable.

Gorilla Characteristics

The largest living primate, gorilla males may reach over 400 pounds (180 kilograms), stand up to 6 feet (2 meters) tall, and possess almost incomprehensible strength. A gorilla can snap a bamboo trunk 6 inches (15 centimeters) thick in two with as much effort as a man snaps a pencil. Females are smaller, about half the weight and at least a foot shorter than the males.

Gorillas are vegetarians, feeding on over fifty different plant species in some areas. Many of these plants are so moisture rich that adults rarely drink water.

or several females. The silverback is the undisputed leader of his group, and a mere glance is enough to quell disturbances amongst his family, or to provide him first choice at any food source. Unless disturbed, theirs is a quiet, peaceful existence.

Chimpanzees

That's quite a contrast from the second largest African primate, the chimpanzee, which includes the common chimpanzee and the bonobo, or pygmy chimp. Chimps are far more vociferous, and their hoots, barks, screams, pants, and squeals allow them to communicate with one another as they forage.

Chimpanzees live in large, loose communal groups governed by several adult males who patrol their territory. Most territorial disputes are settled by screams and posturing, but lone individuals will be hunted down and attacked, often resulting in serious if not fatal injuries.

Unlike the strictly vegetarian gorilla, chimps eat a variety of foods, including meat when available. Young baboons, colobus monkeys, and the young of small antelope and bushpigs are all potential prey. Immensely adaptable, chimps were one of the first mammals to be observed using tools. They frequently use stems of grass to fish out termites, and some chimps use clubs or rocks to break the hard shells of certain nuts.

Other Primates

In many ways, the baboon resembles the chimp in both social structure and food preference. It too lives in large community groups, called troops, protected by several dominant males. Baboons are found in a variety of habitats, but they're most commonly seen foraging across the savannahs, looking for grasses,

A male olive baboon scratches itself. Insect pests are few as baboons spend several hours each day mutually grooming, eating any ticks, lice, and other pesky insects they find.

Two subspecies exist. Mountain gorillas live in and around the forested mountains, hills, and volcanic peaks of Rwanda, Uganda, and the Congo, and it is this subspecies tourists visit most often. Ironically, despite the tourism, this subspecies is critically endangered due to habitat loss, and to a lesser extent, poaching. The more common lowland gorilla enjoys a more extensive range, extending throughout central and west Africa.

Gorillas live in social groups composed of a dominant male—called a silverback for the grizzled, whitish coat it develops upon maturity—subadult males that are his sons, and one

Chimpanzees eat a variety of foods, including plants and some animal matter. In some locales, male chimpanzees have developed into skillful hunters that seek out monkeys. Kills become the sole property of the chimp who made it; others will gather around, arms outstretched to seek handouts.

Female baboons are very tolerant of each other's young. Curious females often investigate new additions to the troop, even seeking to hold the baby for a few minutes.

roots, nuts, and other edible plants. Like chimpanzees, baboons will eat meat when they have the opportunity.

Group cohesiveness and social order is maintained in two ways: grooming and submission to rank. Baboons spend a great deal of time grooming each other, and although males will groom females, they spend far more of their time being groomed. Social order is easily observed as lower ranked individuals present themselves in a submissive display to dominant ones as they pass.

Several other species of primates inhabit Africa, many of which live in the high forest canopies of western and central Africa, and which are on the endangered species list due to habitat loss and hunting by man. Some of the lesser primates seen more regularly on safari, at least in East Africa, are the blue monkey, the green vervet monkey, and the black-and-white colobus.

The vervet, or green, monkey is the most commonly seen true monkey. Although they normally inhabit acacia woodlands, they are sometimes found far out on the grasslands, hundreds of yards from the nearest tree.

Impalas often associate with baboons, since their presence protects them from the attacks of cheetahs and leopards. They enjoy this protection at a price, as unwary fawns or does are often seized by baboons for food.

FOLLOWING PAGE: Gaboon vipers are one of the most beautiful snakes in Africa. Its cryptic coloration, a patchwork of triangles and stripes, makes it extremely difficult to see on the forest floor where it makes its home.

A Nile crocodile lunges upward to catch a Thompson's gazelle. The gazelle was trying to cross the Mara River in Kenya, when it was ambushed by the crocodile lying in wait in shallow water.

Although a crocodile's mouth is full of teeth it cannot bite chunks of meat from a carcass. Instead, a crocodile bites, then rolls rapidly, literally wrenching chunks of flesh free as it does so.

Crocodiles and Other Reptiles

Of all the African animals, the Nile crocodile is perhaps the most dangerous. They are common throughout Africa, playing a role as both predator and scavenger along most rivers, swamps, and ponds. Villagers fishing or collecting water must be careful; crocodiles will eat anything they can catch.

Although aquatic, crocodiles are tied to the land for nesting. Females dig a nest in a sandy bank where several dozen eggs may be deposited. Unlike many reptiles that ignore their nest or young, female crocodiles actively guard the nest from predators, awaiting the time when the hatchlings announce their arrival by squeaking grunts. Hearing these, the female digs up her nest, freeing her young and often carrying hatchlings down to the safety of the water in her powerful, multi-toothed jaws.

Crocodile-like in their appearance, large lizards belonging to the monitor family often dig up unguarded crocodile nests, feeding on the uppermost eggs or the entire clutch if the female remains away. Along the rivers, the Nile monitor, measuring 6 feet (2 meters) in length), is the most common, but inland in grassy or arid areas the blunt-nosed savanna

The largest reptile in Africa is the Nile crocodile. Large males may reach eighteen feet (5.5 meters) or longer, although their huge girth make them look even larger.

monitor takes its place, often using termite mounds as its home.

In much of Africa, leopard tortoises, some as large as a bushel-basket, plod along on blunt, elephantine legs, feeding on flowers and soft grasses. In the kopjes of Tanzania, pancake tortoises maneuver their flattish shells adapted to slide into the gaps and ledges of the rock. Moss-covered side-necked turtles live in every stream and pond. This primitive group, lacking the S-shaped neck of most turtles and tortoises, protects its head and neck by swinging its neck sideways.

In the arid deserts of Namibia, geckos and shovel-nosed lizards chase insects across the sand. In this oven-hot environment, shovel-nosed lizards often "dance" on two legs, alternately raising their feet to minimize contact with the hot sand. When the heat grows too intense, these lizards seek the shade of isolated shrubs, or burrow a few inches beneath the sand surface.

Chameleons

The most intriguing of Africa's lizards are the chameleons. There are several species, including the triceratops-like, three-horned Jackson, and the common flap-necked chameleon. These creatures are unique. Since their stalk-like eyes can rotate independently, a chameleon can literally look up and down, or front and back, at the same time. They possess a prehensile tail and feet with toes fused together in a pliers like grip. Of course, chameleons change color, but they do so as much to express their mood as they do for camouflage. Perhaps most unique is their method of feeding. Chameleons catch prey with their tongue, which fires from their mouth in a hydraulic extension, sometimes extending almost their entire body's length.

Tree agamas are brilliantly colored. They are rarely seen, seeking the shelter of holes or crevices whenever danger threatens.

Savannah monitors often hide inside large termite mounds. On cool or rainy mornings the monitors often rest just outside their entrance hole.

After feeding upon the clutch of Egyptian geese eggs a Nile monitor yawns. These monitors are at ease on land and in the water, and are adept at climbing trees.

Snakes

Eyes capable of seeing in all directions are handy for a chameleon, for the venomous green mamba is just one of its many predators. The name brings a chill to many safari goers, and grizzled guides often delight in telling stories of angry snakes dropping into tourist vans. They are just stories. Snakes are rarely seen.

Yet Africa is well represented by hundreds of species, including the notorious green mamba, which is a brilliant green; the black mamba, an olive-gray snake whose black mouth lining gives it its name; and puff adders, that explosively hiss and inflate when disturbed. A similar species, the incredibly well camouflaged Gaboon viper, possesses the longest fangs of any snake, over 1.5 inches (3.8 centimeters) in a large adult.

Non-venomous snakes are far more numerous. The largest are the pythons, including the African rock python which grows to about twenty feet and is capable of catching prey the size of impala or leopards.

Pythons are constrictors, grabbing hold of their victim with a lightning-fast bite using jaws equipped with scores of fish-hook like teeth. Instantly, the snake coils itself over its prey, then continues to do so until the prey is wrapped in a series of ever tightening coils. Contrary to popular belief, they do not crush the bones of their prey. Instead, the coils tighten until the animal, its ribcage compressed, stops breathing.

Perhaps the most bizarre feeding behavior is that of the tiny egg-eating snake. Only about two feet long, this small snake feeds on the eggs of small birds. It seems impossible that the snake can swallow a round object several times the size of its head, but by securing a grip with its small teeth, the snake works the egg down into its throat. There, special bones in its neck vertebrae are employed, and as the snake contracts, the egg is forced against these bony projections to shatter the eggshell. The liquid contents are swallowed, and the now useless shell regurgitated.

Perhaps the most common venomous snake is the stocky puff adder. It gets its name from its hissing, puffing display.

For obvious reasons, the rainbow-colored lilac-breasted roller is a favorite for travelers on safari. Rollers get their name from the spectacular aerial acrobatics displayed during courtship, when birds literally tumble through the air before pulling out into a glide just meters above the ground.

Feathered Rainbows

While many visit Africa intent on seeing the large mammals, the diversity and color of the continent's bird life comes as an unexpected surprise. This variety is astounding: in size, in color, and in the wealth of adaptations and shapes exhibited. There are ostriches 7 feet (2 meters) tall, tiny colorful kingfishers less than 5 inches (12 centimeters) in length,

The saddle-billed stork is the most vividly colored of the African storks. Although males and females look similar, they can be identified by their eyes. The males eyes are brown, the females yellow.

rainbow-hued lilac-breasted rollers, red carmine bee-eaters, giant ground hornbills, and cryptic nightjars and stone curlews. Approximately 8,000 species of birds inhabit this planet, and of these, 1,800 or so live or migrate through Africa. Almost 1,100 species have been recorded in Kenya and Tanzania alone.

As would be expected, this plethora of bird life exploits an equally vast range of ecological niches. Red-billed and yellow-billed oxpeckers hike up the necks of giraffes, disappear into the ears of rhinos, or dip into the flaring nostrils of buffaloes, seeking fat ticks and fur lice, often combing through stiff hairs by a scissors action of their bills.

Curious Nesters

To brood their young, hornbills of several species imprison the females in tree cavities, enclosing them inside their nest until the eggs hatch. Both males and females collaborate in this procedure, gathering up mud or dung to form a plastered wall that dries and hardens in the sun. The male feeds his entombed mate through a small opening in the wall. When the hatchlings are old enough, she breaks out of the cavity, which the young promptly reseal until only a small opening remains, to assist her mate in securing food for the growing chicks.

Weavers of a variety of colors and sizes construct intricate nests that hang from trees on long braided strands, often at the tips of slender branches. Many start by weaving a stout circle of grasses, then embellish this into nests of funnels, sacks, or bags, often in such density that limbs break from their combined weight. Seemingly suspended in mid-air, the nests are often safe from marauding monkeys, most snakes, and other bird-eating predators.

One of a pair of red-billed hornbills investigates a tree cavity at the start of the rainy season. If the pair find it suitable, the male will imprison the female inside until after her eggs hatch by walling off the opening with mud and dung. A small vertical slit in the wall will allow the male to continue feeding his mate during this period.

Yellow-billed hornbills are found in many arid areas. They await the rainy season to collect mud to build their nests.

One of the most beautiful birds in Africa is the crowned crane. It is the national bird of Uganda.

Some Typical Species

In the grasses below, long-legged secretary birds patrol for prey. Secretary birds are best known for their snake hunting ability, but in truth these reptiles play only a small role in their diet. Their unusual name was once thought to be derived from the bird's head plumes which resembled the feathered pens scribes used in the late 1800s, but more likely the Arabic name for this bird, *Saqret-tair*, or hunter bird, stuck because of the similarity of pronunciation.

In arid areas sandgrouse visit waterholes daily. It's said that bushmen, knowing the time of day a sandgrouse drinks, can pinpoint the direction and distance to unknown waterholes by observing the sandgrouse's flight. At the waterholes, male sandgrouse both drink and dip their breast feathers in the pools. When the sandgrouse returns to the nesting area, water adhering to these breast feathers is sipped by his young. Interestingly, females do not collect water for the young.

In the marshlands and swamps, long-toed African jacanas literally walk across the water, using their prodigious digits to displace their weight upon the water plants they walk on. Storks of a variety of sizes and colors share these wetlands, including the distinctive black and white saddle-billed stork, distinguished

In many bird species, the physical characteristics of the sexes differ. The male of the paradise flycatcher has a long trailing tail, the female does not.

by a red bill banded by black and capped by a bright yellow "saddle" at its base. In winter, thousands of European storks fly to African grasslands and savannas to hunt insects, sometimes gathering in immense flocks when grass fires drive prey from cover. The most frequently seen stork is the common Marabou, a feisty scavenger that circles the edge of kills, picking up scraps or stealing from vultures hopping by with unswallowed morsels.

Along the rivers in southern Africa, huge colonies of white-fronted and carmine bee-eaters nest, burrowing their nest holes in steep banks where their young are safe from hungry snakes. In arid areas, the tiny Somalian bee-eater nests directly in the ground.

Bee-eaters, as their name would imply, catch bees and other flying insects. Alone or in small flocks, the birds perch, watching with quick

Although a ground hunter, secretary birds nest in trees, usually preferring flat-toped acacias twenty feet (6 meters) or more off the ground.

moves of their head every insect that flies by. They are remarkably agile, launching themselves and catching their prey mid-air, often to return to the same perch where the birds beat the insect upon the limb before swallowing.

No trip to Africa would seem complete without seeing an ostrich, the world's largest bird. They are dimorphic, with males a study in black and white, and females a drab gray-brown. Although flightless, ostriches employ their wings in courtship displays, where they dip and wiggle, tossing their wings out in elaborate fan dances. Several females may lay their eggs in a single nest which one male helps guard. If all the eggs hatch, surviving the jaws of hyenas or the destructive feet of curious elephants, as many as fifty tiny chicks may be seen scurrying behind a pair of ostriches as they strut across the savanna.

There are two subspecies of ostrich, the Masai and the Somalian. Although females look alike, the males differ, with the Masai having a red neck and legs, and the Somalian having a blue neck and thighs. These colors are most evident during the breeding season.

Afterword

Imagine that tomorrow, on some remote Pacific island, a population of living dinosaurs was discovered; that animals thought to be extinct for seventy million years still existed. Imagine the excitement shared by scientists and the general public, and the efforts that would be made to make sure that this island would be protected and conserved, so that this remnant of the past was not forever lost.

Well, that's not going to happen, but in a very real sense we are faced with a very similar situation today with the wildlife of Africa. Sadly, this world wildlife treasure is in danger of extermination, as populations rise, and as wild lands are converted to farmland and human living space. Each year, in areas throughout Africa, wildlife ministries and park managers are pressured by outside forces to give up land, relinquish needed park-generated revenues, or control animal populations that are deemed competitive to man or viewed as an economic commodity. Worse still, political instability and ecoterrorism have, at this time, effectively removed some of the premiere wildlife viewing areas from most tourists' itineraries. Without tourist revenues, the parks and refuges in these areas, and the wildlife they contain, are in imminent danger.

The wildlife of Africa is more than a regional treasure. It is of global significance, which, if lost, will be gone forever. Continued support for conservation organizations is one of the ways that those who care about wildlife can ensure the survival of this wonderful resource.

As grass fires flush out insects, mice, and small reptiles, migrating European storks gather by the thousands during their migration through Africa to feed upon the bounty.

A male black-headed wearver alertly perches on a branch. Just above him is the elaborately woven nest which he has constructed and in which his mate will incubate her eggs and care for her young.

INDEX

*Page numbers in **bold-face** type indicate photo captions.*